HEAVEN WE HAVEN'T YET DREAMED

Heaven We Haven't Yet Dreamed

poems by

Dianne Borsenik
Juliet Cook
Puma Perl
Jeanette Powers

Stubborn Mule Press
Devil's Elbow, MO
stubbornmulepress.com

All poems copyright 2019 to the poet of origin
© Borsenik, Cook, Perl, Powers

First Edition 11 7 5 3 2 1
ISBN: 978-1-950380-58-9
LCCN: 2019948884
Design, edits and layout: Jeanette Powers
stubbornmulepress@gmail.com @stubbornmulepress
Edits: Linzi Garcia
Back Cover Author Photo Credits: John Burroughs (Dianne Borsenik); Juliet Cook, self; Len DeLessio (Puma Perl); Nathanael William Stolte (Jeanette Powers)
Interior Art: "The Moon Card" by Jeanette Powers

Are you really reading this? Congratulations, we love you. No one but the author can really claim rights to their work, no matter what law says what. And we can't really do anything about theft, whatever that means, so here is our pact: Be cool, be kind, don't steal, email the author if you like or want to riff off their work. Also, let us at Stubborn Mule know if you want to write a review, we'll share it and your review publication, too. Go ahead and use passages for reviews, accolades, or epigraphs, give credit where credit is due. Let's stay radical, share with us our honor among anarchists.

Cover Art:
Alone at Night, by Amy Scherer
find more of Scherer's work at arthousestudio.org

BORSENIK Contents

Celsius
Spring Fever
Anomalies in the Garden
Infinite Corners
Aurora Borealis
Ecliptic
Communion
Sticks
Incontrovertible
Driven: A Play in Five Parts
Classical Gas
Bohemian Rhapsody
Piece of My Heart
Of What
Wearing Mail
Psalmodies in Vitro
Fall Out
Fahrenheit

COOK Contents

Batter Up
Doll Blood Spattering
Unfriend Everyone
What Good Does the Truth Do?
I Need to Bow My Head ...
Families ...
My Tendency ...
Not a Member ...
Flying Snake
Dark Light
When I Was a Little Girl ...
Bloodlines
Out of Control
Dropping Point
Root Rot
You Pull Your Latest ...
Ripped out Red

Inside an Old Basement
Maybe She Doesn't Exist Anymore

PERL Contents

Poetry
Where I'm From ...
Youngblood Sister ...
Here Is What You Don't Know
Walls
For Annie
Final Frontiers
Waves of New York Poets
And Still Just There
Leonard Cohen Inspirations
End of the World

POWERS Contents

Water Is a Woman
Newton's Second Law
Hearts Break All the Time
Reflections in the Windows of Your First Car
Brother D
Delta Heart Equals Zero
Run Away with the Circus
Snippets of Poems that Didn't Make It into Poems
How We Move on
Some Quick of Hope
95 is Still an A
Never Turn Down a Glass of Sweet Tea
Old Dogs
Sister, Sing Me
Cycles of Grief Go on and on
After Bouguereau's *The Bathers*

Dianne
Borsenik

Celsius
      —July 4, 2019, Ohio

An unusual heat wave is smothering
large swaths of the country, with mussels
steaming in their shells in California,
and roads in South Dakota buckling
from the stress. Alaska hits 90°, an all-time
high. The heat dome extends to Europe—
France feels a spike to 115°. CNN wonders
if parts of India have become too hot to be
inhabitable...too hot for humans. Climate
change lawsuits against corporate interests
and governments are spreading around
the world, with the U. S. as global leader
in climate change litigation.

A hospital patient recovering from pneumonia
goes for a walk-while-black and is arrested—
too obvious, the theft of the IV tubing taped
to his arm, the medicine gravitied to his vein.
The police have to remove his IV to apply
the handcuffs. Dr. Martin Luther King, Jr. said
"No one is free until we are all free." Border
children in U. S. custody are drawing pictures
of cages—they believe they're in jail.
Forty-five tweets "If immigrants are unhappy
with the conditions in the...detention centers,
just tell them not to come." None of Forty-
five's grandparents were born in the U. S., nor
did they speak English as their mother tongue.

There are tanks on the National Mall this
scorcher of a Fourth, presaging the "rockets'
red glare" and the "bombs bursting in air"
in the night ahead. In a salute to (the potency
of) the country's armed forces, flyovers of

fighter jets are scheduled. Various members of the military brass have expressed concern about politicization of the holiday. Veterans pass out t-shirts in support of the USS John McCain. McCain, a war hero and Republican Senator, still is ridiculed almost a year after his death by the President of his country. Forty-five tweets "We own the planes... we own the tanks and all." There's a fifty percent chance of storms forming directly over the capital.

This morning, local weathermen report northern Ohio will continue to be very humid with a chance of a few afternoon raindrops. Temps may top out at around 90°—just like in Alaska. That's Fahrenheit. Large swaths of the country may be mentally translating the number to 32°—the Celsius scale is used by all countries except Liberia, the Bahamas, the Caymans, Belize, and the United States of America.

Spring Fever

Above, absinthe-chartreuse vernal fuzz,
below, blanket bed of mossy fecundity.
Carried on the breeze, celestial scent of sex
driving biodiversity to deliver the goods, however or whatever it takes, planned or improv,
farm-fresh or citified. Shy fumblings, *amour fou*,
guilty pleasures, the casual lay, all called to riot
here in these months of tillage and seeds,
in this season that welcomes the return of solar
juju. Earth, dropping her robes, opens the *suq*,
kisses her patrons on both cheeks. *Come, shop
love in this moment*, she says, and her heart's tattoo
mines the night with little torpedoes of passion.

Anomalies in the Garden

What are the questions
that snake widdershins
around the calyx
of sentience?
When does the antiphon begin?
    Where
        is it written—
is it coiled, cabalistic,
in the genome?
Isn't it enough
    that a chest
    must be content with
imperfect anima, animus,
the percussion
of anomalies in the Om?
    Only one
harvest is forbidden.
Chemistry
confounds the
    heart;
    the rhythms
of dubiety, transgression,
buffet the whorl
    of two
helices in ascending dance,
jar the tarantella
of two
    hearts beating
in deliquescence,
foreordained.
Orison, orison, orison; be
    as one.
Why can't we conjure
this certainty?
Blame it on ophidian apocrypha.

    Ah, that's the music—
Kaddish sung over glial framework
of aubergine, cyan, the bruised nativity
    of life.

Infinite Corners
      —after "Fractal," a bowl-shaped piece of art
            by William Montgomery

Om.
Orison.
Ouroboros.

Origin.
Oracle.
Orgasm.

This is the shape of our Mother Earth;
this is the shape of birth.
This is the sacred geometry.
This is the Golden Mean—
the Fibonacci sequence, spiraling to infinity.
From flower to fractal to nautilus shell,
from hurricane to galaxy to human cell,
the infinite corners of Pi piece it together.

Open.
Other.
Ophiuchus.

Om.
Orison.
Ouroboros.

This is the sacred geometry.
This is the holy plan.
This is the sum of all the parts—,
the infinite corners
of Woman and of Man.

Aurora Borealis

What are these waveforms of energy
and where will they lead?
Gravity hugs me to this planet,
magnetic forces align me.
I am an iron filing pointing to the True North.
Metallic taste of lightning tickles my lips,
my fingers curl around bits of starstuff.
I feel atoms dancing on my palm.

Ecliptic

—after a photograph in Casey Rearick's
"Inference: Anxiety, Sensuality, Tension"
series

Not wind, an outside force,
causing the concealment; no,

not the movement of the world
in which she's contained. Her

body finds torque and zodiac,
the shifting of planets, inside,

and motivates the whip. Eyes
are not to be read, nor smile, nor

frown. Thousands of filaments
will say what's to be said: *I am*

filled with blazing constellations
and this is mine; you are denied.

Communion
> *—3525 Liberty Avenue*
> *Pittsburgh, PA*

on the way we've been detoured
to the poetry reading
we spot The Church Brew Works
and he says *it's a sign from god*
so of course we park the car
enter, find our pew, and order
holy communion

The Donald Mexican Lime Lager
and
Pipe Organ Pale Ale

the spirit of hops compels us

Sticks
*—5801 Detroit Ave.
Cleveland, Ohio*

*Happy Dog
Live Music
Good Food*

neon stains the sidewalks
as the four of us slouch
at carside, all eyes on
the drummer's hands
as he peels a joint
from a box of
white sticks, the joking
"Don't toke a Q-tip"
and laughter, "Let's see
where we can go" and slipping
around the back of the building
where lack of line of sight
and lack of light is enough
for four stick shadows
to suck it in
and pass it to the right

Incontrovertible

Rules of the road trip in summer:
Burn
rubber.
Top
down.
Burn
gas.
Grin.
Sun-
burn
of summer rules! Trip the road. In.

Driven: A Play in Five Parts

1.
He will plan the trip
and ask if she'd like to go with him.
She will gladly accept his invitation.
He will pull in the driveway.
She will have high hopes.
It will be comfortable for a few miles.
She will be excited to be with him;
she will feel on top of the world.
After a time, she will notice
he seems somewhat distracted.
She will try to engage him.
He will appear disinterested in talking.
He will turn up the radio.
She will ask what's wrong.
He will tell her she's imagining things.
He will tell her everything's okay.

2.
They will arrive at the hotel.
She will press for attention.
He will become defensive.
She will wonder why he invited her.
He will accuse her of spoiling the mood.
She will grow insecure.
She will beg him to lighten up.
He will tell her she's the problem.
She will begin to cry.
He will be angry.
They will argue.
She will wish aloud
that she hadn't come on the trip.
He will retort that he wished
he'd never invited her.

He will withdraw.
She will internalize.

3.
He will finally relent and suggest dinner.
She will put on fresh makeup.
They will go out and act
as if nothing bad had happened.
They will eat and drink
and return to their room.
He will reach for her.
She will hunger.
They will make love.
They will not cuddle afterward.

4.
He will awaken and make coffee.
She will attempt a bright conversation.
He will bring up yesterday's events.
She will be confused.
He will be sarcastic.
She will suggest a fresh start.
He will escalate the tension between them.
She will be fearful of another argument.
She will be conciliatory.
He will tell her that she
doesn't want him to be happy.
Desperate, she will apologize.
And apologize.
He will, after an extended pause
of time, accept.
He will reach for her again.
She will try to please him.

5.
They will leave on their return journey.
She will be careful not to provoke him.
He will smile at her.
He will drop her off and drive home.
She will post on social media a photo of the trip captioned "It was great!"
He will hit ♥ on it.

Classical Gas
>—after "Classical Gas," *oil painting by Dave King*
>—after "Classical Gas," *song by Mason Williams*

Of two worlds, of two separate energies,
yin and yang, animus and anima,
driven from the distant past
into the present by classic fossil fuels
and the divine spark of electricity,
hipster, groover, rebel to all that's Right,
Left to all that's important, squinting
against the sunlight but facing tomorrow
head-on, the music in his head a crescendo
of past lives, people, and the inevitability
of change, all becoming orgasm,
the defining moment of a generation.

Bohemian Rhapsody
    —for John Dorsey

Red-haired Viking warrior brother,
not of the blood but of the heart,
shorter than I but taller in so many ways,
two-fisted poet quaffing experience like
Old Overholt rye, belting out your life
to an audience held captive by your passion,
street to street, city to city, a vagabond
traveling the lines to the next café,
the next dive bar, the next encounter,
the next chapter in your newest book.

Remember that time in Cincinnati when
a whole room of strangers sang the words
to "Bohemian Rhapsody," unprompted
and in full sync? You were fierce then,
my brother, your red beard full of laughter
and love, you, my brother, closer to me than
my sister—an only child—ever was.

Piece of My Heart
    —for Jeanette Powers

I'm not sure why, but they remind
me of Janis Joplin, balls-out and bluesy,
unafraid to face the world on their terms,
comfortable in their skin, a force of nature,
ink in one hand and paint in the other,
their blue, blue eyes melting permafrost.

When I first met them I wanted to read them,
tattoos spilling from them like the aurora
borealis, their soul slicking the outside of their
body, ablaze with color, as they swept me along
with them to pull the stars down from heaven.

I type another little piece of my heart
and it comes out another little piece of my heat—
oh, yes. That suits them better. They burn.

Of What
  —for Alex Gildzen

Of what
are those special
moments that
intensify our
days? Lavender
socks walked
him down
San Franciscan
streets to meet
a movie star—
a dream from
the sixties,
when icons
signed photos
and sent them
to adoring
and adorable
young men
in Ohio.

Of what
are those special
moments that
make art of our
days? Lavender
socks walked
him home,
where he
discovered
poetry in
the absence
of a few threads
of cotton,
beauty in

his need for
it, and a certain
kind of keeping
in the act of
giving away.

Wearing Mail
>   —after *"Priority Male Dress Shirt 2018,"*
>   paper mailing envelopes by Deborah Sementelli

\<Male\> wearing hauberk
\<Mail\> bearing torso
Priority \<Male\>
Chain \<Mail\> Delivery

Shirt
Old Frankish word "halsberg"
becomes "bergen," meaning
to save
to rescue
to give protection
to the throat, the neck

Poet
interlocking loops of mettle
a construct making ah, more
to say
to produce
to be creation
from the throat, the neck

Service required, and postage

Thank you thank you thank you
for choosing (you sing) Mr. \<Mail\>

Psalmodies in Vitro

Who will pour
the vial of psalmody
upon the whorled
diaspora of
    stars,
who will consecrate
the placenta
of Canicula, who
will kindle
the annealing
    glow in the black
throat of the apocalypse?
When will the paean
begin?
Ave, ave,
calyx, cotyledon,
the viridian
anima that beatifies
harvest, the animus
that shellacs
abalone
    lake of sky.
    As the full
tessellation manifests,
transgressions reveal.
The crux is Time. The
    moon makes
hibernaculum against
threnody, ululation
of stones. Reprieve
wends
    its slow way
    through this
rugose landscape,
slides over *mare,*

coils, gelid, in
crater. What is a
 world without
 color
but a hiccup
in the continuum,
a *caesura*, where
 all time stops
 and we can say
 yes to our
extant names,
christened by
the redolent attar of
 dreams,
pale, luciferous,
beautiful.

Fall Out

As summer slowly fizzles, autumn's showy waltz
begins its all too brief and duplicitous sway.
Cleveland knows its time is short. Polar vortex
dominates the horizon, a season where wheelbarrow
evolves into snowplow, walking becomes improv.
Forget bare feet and flip-flops; hello, flu.

Goodbyes loom, so this last dance is bittersweet;

hearts grow heavy as a steamy solar romance fades.
Ice and snow will tyrannize for months. Cross-over,
jalopy, sedan, tuner, truck, might as well be umiaq
kiting the Northern waterways. But before leaf-crisp
launches into crust-crunch, fall twirls, *pianissimo*,
moving across the floor of Ohio, away from the sun.

Fahrenheit
—January 30, 2019
—after Josh Brooks

Yesterday, he said his
nipples could cut glass,
and that's how cold it is

this morning. Windchills
are currently minus
twenty-six, and dropping

steadily throughout the day.
All the news channels are
talking about an "arctic

blast" moving in a swath
across the States, with
the winds in our region

gusting at thirty miles
per hour. Tomorrow
should be a little better,

and the seven-day outlook
is insane, with temps
climbing into the fifties

on Tuesday. But today,
it's nipples-cutting-glass
frosty, and I'm braless.

It looks like I'm going to
need some new shirts,
come this weekend.

Juliet
Cook

Batter Up

There was a large circle of chairs with female poet bodies sitting on top of them.

They were having a conversation, preceding a yes or no vote, about whether or not a poem of mine should be removed from a source that had already chosen to publish it.

Chosen or not, some questions were now being raised. It had come to some gender-based assumptions that I was not the kind of feminist they had thought I was, because I had mutant pigs as friends.

They no longer wanted to publish a poem by a possible mutant pig breading chick, unless she broke bread with the primary editorial staff members too.

"Do you know what primary staff members are?" that one whispered into my ear. "Do you know how powerful they are? Do you know how they taste?"

The voting panel looked like they were leaning towards pulling me out, but first they wanted me and another female body to share one chair together while they counted backwards from 10 to 0.

I was supposed to sit on her lap and the two of us were told to make competitive oinking sounds after every number until we hit 0. Then it was time to start running.

Perpetually racing around the circle of chairs in a cakewalk competition in which all the baked cakes were shaped like pigs and the winning chick would be hit in the head with a pig cake and then sold to the highest bidder.

How did I get myself into this cake hole? Who do they think they are? Who do they think I am?

Who do I think I am? I think my little mutant pigs are something more than just soft cake batter pig shapes to be cut into edible eatables.

Do they really think I'm not going to rip out their fake fucking pig tails and let the blood drip all over the pig cake frosting and then throw that cake bowl down on the ground and run away from this encircling game and grow my own pig ears?

Doll Blood Spattering

Doll cadavers growing mildew for hair,
mildew spewing out their mouths and whose
voice are they talking in now?

They were talking in their own tiny tongues until
those tiny tongues were ripped out
and replaced with more modern doll mouths.

The modern dolls with no genuine voices of their own.
The modern dolls in a popularity contest, fighting against
every other doll. They don't really care who they hurt.

They don't really care what they're fighting for,
as long as they win the contest and can claim
the latest prize. Another set of fake doll eyes.

Another big glowing dick to swallow
and replace the last one they lied to.
Or a fragile tiny dick to bite off and chew

into contorted pieces and spit the debris
all around in a violently fast group attack.
Anyone who disagrees with these modern dolls

or who doesn't choose to take sides
deserves to be hacked into bloody smithereens
and tossed down the garbage disposal.

This modern doll group is better than everyone else.
Even if their doll brains are evil, mean-spirited, laced
with fake frosting and more dirty than rats.

Even if their doll group agenda is to secretly slink
their long doll tails behind the back of their fancy frilled skirts,
load those tails with venom, then use them to lash out,

to slash out the hearts of individual dolls who don't fit in to their scene. If one of these modern dolls offers you a smile and uses the word love in your face, it is fake.

Love love love love love love love has been programmed into their pretty rotten doll teeth and used to screw with reality and make real love obsolete.

Unfriend Everyone

If you don't make the same choices as me, then please just unfriend me.

If you don't see the same as me,
if you don't act the same as me,
if you don't talk the same as me,
if you don't walk in the same direction as me,
if you don't feel the same way as me,
then just unfriend me.

If you don't agree with me
that Trump's penis is as tiny as a mini wrecking ball
that deserves to be cut
into bite size pieces and rammed
into a scalding hot stew pot, unfriend me.

If you don't agree that every penis is evil
and all men deserve to rot, unfriend me.
If you don't agree that all women are just body parts
with penetrative holes, unfriend me
and watch those hissing pussies burn in hell
and then volcanically explode into your eye balls.

If you don't believe in heaven and hell, then unfriend me before I die.

If you're a Republican, unfriend me.
If you voted for Trump's little dick, un-fucking-friend me.
If you're a Democrat who doesn't have the exact same extremities as me,
just fucking unfriend me too, because you're too unwieldy.

If you don't know how to make a high end screwdriver,
unfriend me, even though I don't know what a high end screwdriver is
and I'm fine with cheap as long as the cheap isn't you.

If you're an Independent free thinker
whose liberal ideas slightly diverge from my liberal ideas,

then just unfriend me you clueless prick. How dare you
not fit in to the specific details of my own unique group.

If you don't like to attack other groups, unfriend me and cut
off a finger.
If you don't like to attach other individuals, unfriend me and
rip out a tooth
and cut off your own damned tongue.
If you're not a fan of alternative cheerleader group attacks,
then what is your mouth good for anyway?

If you don't unfriend the same person that I unfriend,
then you'd better just unfriend ME.
Because I don't want to be friends with ANYONE
who doesn't 100% agree with ME
and approach everything exactly the same as ME
versus YOU versus ME versus YOU versus ME.

If you don't agree with my breast implants, unfriend me.
If you think I deserved to be raped
because afterwards I didn't handle myself
exactly the same way as you thought I should,
because I wasn't as blatantly, straightforwardly, anti male as
you,
then suck my nonexistent dick and unfriend me, because I
already think for myself
that it was partly my own fucking fault for not wearing panties
while walking to work on the weekend.

If you think I'm an over thinker,
if you think I'm an over drinker,
if you think I'm not academic enough
to meet your stupid standards.
If you think I'm an over eater,
if you think my body is too big
or too small to bow down
to your land of model-like conformity,
unfriend me and buy me a breast reduction

or another breast implant surgery and then
unfriend my misaligned nipples.

If you don't want to hear too much
about what I have to say
and would rather just delete and escape
from imperfect contradictory attempts at personal expression,
and quickly attack those who think/act/feel differently than you,
then just keep on unfriending everyone
who doesn't succumb to swallowing
your agendized rules of perfection.

Unfriend everyone because no one is the same as you.
Unfriend everyone until nobody is left but you.

What Good Does the Truth Do?

What do you do when you find out
that trying your best to be honest
just ruins everything?

The fakers seem to score the most points
and gain ongoing momentum and power
to continually increase the stash of their own fake truth serums
shoved into a hidden closet full of pockets full of pills
bitten in half behind your back and then swallowed like candy.

Do you join the crowd of fake and grow a whole sweet arsenal
of sticky secrets leading towards your latest secret fan base?
Or do you just quit expressing yourself to anyone
except for inside your own head? Do you refuse to tell
what you really mean, how you really feel,

who you really are to yourself or to anyone else?
Does the real you even exist?
Maybe nobody really cares anyway.

I Need to Bow My Head and Say Your Prayers Even if I Don't Believe in You

Not liking this day makes me feel ungrateful
but I don't like Easter
or any other group holiday.
They remind me of not fitting into the group.
They make me think I should fit into a group
even if I do not want to.

They remind me of male conversation feeling like nothing
but yelling at the TV screen and taking sides
based on sports teams.
They remind me of female conversation feeling like nothing
but yelling at the kids, telling the kids what to do,
what not to do, where to sit, don't sit on Grandpa's
lazy boy recliner! Only him and his wiener are allowed to sit there!

I'm not allowed to wear that because Grandpa won't like it.
I have way too much makeup on and I need to take it off
and I need to take my clothes off right now
and change myself to fit into the group
even if I do not want to.
I need to learn to be grateful for what I do not want.

Families Are Not Always the Ultimate Dream Team

Sometimes they are rabbit holes full of bitchy rituals
created by women posing as witches
wearing rabbit heads.

They all want to be in charge, but instead
of taking turns talking, their mouths continually hurl out
hailstorms of competitive interruptions.

They tear each other's tails off,
piss all over each other's faces,
and act like their piss is another magic spell.

My Tendency to Feel as If Expressing Myself Is Wrong

My tendency to apologize when I haven't done anything wrong
other than accidentally hurting the feelings of someone
who doesn't understand my feelings.

My tendency to feel like a hissing venomous snake
when the reason I hissed is because my own space was invaded
with mouths that can't stop themselves from approaching me their way.

They don't get me, or they don't see me, or they want to change me,
stomp me down into their so-called solidity,
but I can't suddenly turn off my own venom

or turn it into vanilla snack pack pudding. I can't
cut my own shape, size, and texture or shrink myself
into something with no mouth of its own.

My tendency to secrete too much
bile inside myself. My self-
deprecation of my own contorting thoughts.

Part of me thinking maybe I should just let them
remove all my skin with unreal depilatory cream;
break down my sharp teeth into holey.

Not a Member of Your Snake Handling Church Organ

I want someone to love the way I am now
rather than hear someone insinuate I used to be better
in the past. More balanceable, smaller, younger.
More willing to be surrounded by hissing snakes.

Those who will never stop hissing behind my back,
I want to move their extended tongues away from me
and my cluttered open space. I refuse to lock every piece of me
behind closed doors so they don't have to look or think
about the current me and can just keep on backtracking

to back when I was easier to control. That was the past.
They can choose to interpret themselves.
They can interpret me their own way too, but
they can't tone me down or tidy me up.
So what if I am the opposite
of their dream?

Flying Snake

What I need is a pair of thigh highs with snakes on them.
Last month, I felt like I looked old and unattractive,
but this month, I feel like I look like a young attractive snake.

I know some people wouldn't insert
the words "young" and "attractive" next to a snake
(or the word "snake" as a comparison for a human face,
but maybe those people haven't seen my face yet).
I know some people wouldn't manage to cheer
themselves up from a funeral home procession
by starting to write a few lines about their upset thoughts
and then turning it into a poem that turned themselves
into a snake, but now I feel less depressed and less clichéd.

Now I feel more okay about my own contorted thinking
and more like a woman who needs snakes on her legs,
one half poisonous; the other half sweet.

Dark Light

Coughing Anne Sexton out of my mouth
in a flaming sneeze filled with fire and light
to bring the depressed and deceased back
to life. Then I will hang her tiny head
stuck to facial tissue on top of the
refrigerator until her head grows
large enough to create a new vase.

Then her body will emerge from the incinerator.
Ashes will turn into dark flowered trees.
New eyes will open inside the branches.

When I Was a Little Girl, I Threw a Rock at a Crab and Accidentally Killed It

A tiny lime green creature crawls out
from underneath a tiny doll house carapace
and hisses. A tiny red baby sticks its head out
from underneath the bed. Inside the pillow,
something tries to shake itself into my head.
The bedroom light bulbs turn into doll heads.
Perennial bulbs that open and shut their mouths,
depending on whether the light is on or off.
Sometimes the light stays on for a very long time,
flickering in different directions, as though
it might break or explode before I can turn it off.

Bloodlines

I fantasized about barbed wire.

I grew up sheltered, strung
in between other people's pieces,
so overprotected I felt the need to rip myself out

through a jagged fence
in order to see for myself,
name my own blood.

Then I started flooding
in too many different directions,
unable to control my own flow.

I didn't want to be rigid,
but I didn't know what I wanted
so I bent into all sorts of drenched shapes.

I ripped out every list of directions and lost it.

Out of Control

Like an insectile heart eater,
filled with blood and guilt.
I didn't mean to bite
or swallow, but sometimes

we can't resist our unaligned cravings.
My weaknesses outweighed
my own strengths again or
maybe it was the other way around.

You didn't really deserve me on top
of you. I didn't deserve to be born
this way, unable to shut my own mouth,
filled with an ongoing expanse of stingers.

No control except for someone else
temporarily holding my hands down.
My own spiked sex appeal,
a gun firing itself into nothing.

Dropping Point

We tone our own misery down
until we hardly even care
about anything.

It's better to tone my thighs
instead of thinking
about who will die next.

The scale says I've lost three more pounds,
too bad I still want another drink
to replace my anxiety with more buzzing.

I can't control the bees, growing into
an escalating swarm,
stingers aiming towards my half-dead heart,

the other half diving underneath
the boiling point until it sizzles.
Blistered flesh with bulging blue veins,
swollen belly, my wasted brain.

Root Rot

My clavicles are turning
into grim reapers inside me.
They want to pierce their way through
my own dying skin.

Sometimes I can't ascertain my taste
buds and why they want
to rip out my seedy tongue.
Replace it with acidic marmalade vomit.

My whole body will be engulfed
by bitter oranges, rotting oleander
that still drips, an ongoing cataclysm of poison
flower bed abortion.

You Pull Your Latest Force Field out and Shoot Another Load

You're forceful.
You tend to talk over me
as soon as I disagree
with anything you have to say.

As soon as I escape
into my own space and think
my own thoughts
at my own pace,

I realize
your attempt
to maroon me
to force yourself upon me
with breakneck invasion.

You want to make me want
what you want for yourself,
because you know you are always right
and anyone who disagrees with YOU
is a total asshole
because you you you you YOU.

You can't stop jacking off
your intense self-entitled prick.
Anyone who disagrees with that hot hard on,
must have a vendetta against YOU.

So what if you're the one stabbing barbs
against countless unwilling backs;
cutting closed mouths open with blades.

Your blood screams out sudden and mean
because you're a REAL prick, fully erect
and you know they all deserve it,
every dripping dropping blobbing red
hot minute of your latest jab.

Ripped out Red

I thought I had managed to escape your grip
by locking you out. I found out locks don't block you;
they enrage you and make you more forceful.
You pounded and kicked open the door,
screaming. You flung me into the bathtub then pulled me out
screaming. You flung me down.

I screamed until my eyes popped, my ear drums broke,
my hair flew all over the room into almost oblivion
except for the screaming and you pounding me
into a broken prop. You poured red paint into my body.
You flung the red paint all over the bathroom floor
until I couldn't scream my own voice out anymore.
My mouth sounded like a red gurgling toilet.

You left me gurgling down on the hard ground,
red flushed cracked handles,
a broken jack o' lantern floating somewhere
up there in some part of what used to be
a ceiling, a fan base I never wanted to see
breaking down from the frames, all around
me and my ribs, my ripped uncovered red parts.

Inside an Old Basement

My tongue was pulled out of my mouth.
A red tongue bath
staining an old box.

Broken lights.
Broken bulbs.
Broken glass.

Another broken light blue egg.
Nobody loves you he said.
You might as well suck
the dead baby
bird out.

What did I think he wanted anyway?
Nobody wants all of me.
They just want small pieces.

Tear another part out,
stick it in
another box.
Nobody will look inside
after the blood dries.

Maybe She Doesn't Exist Anymore

She lives in the controlled horror
of this nursing home.
She is trapped inside
the room of her slow demise.
She lost her spouse.
She lost her cat.
She lost her hearing.
She lost her sight.
She lost her joy in life
and wishes she was dead already.

Did she kill her cat?
She must have done something bad,
because she's lost most of her visitors.

She can't remember who
the other ones are.
She can't remember her name.
She keeps her mouth shut
so she doesn't lose her tongue
or has it already been cut out?
She usually keeps her eyes closed,
because she's not sure what she's looking at
or how she looks inside
anybody else's mind.

Nobody wants to hold her hand.
She wonders if maybe she didn't pet
her cat enough and so it stopped moving.
She wonders if maybe she didn't give
her cat enough treats
and that's why it left her.

Maybe if they would have given her
one more chance to cook dinner,

but she doesn't have any ingredients left,
she doesn't have her own kitchen,
and all the guests are gone.

All she has is a chair and a bed
and it feels like a never ending grave that nobody visits.

Puma Perl

Poetry

This is Poetry. This is not Poetry.
Wear a black see-through shirt
and a red laced bra.
You don't wear red bras beneath
black see-through shirts.
Unbutton the shirt. Never unbutton.
This is Poetry. This is not Poetry.

There is no such thing as monogamy.
Only denial.
I shouldn't know what I know.
It's not Poetry.
My thigh high stockings fall down.
It's Poetry.

And the beautiful poets are everywhere.
The smart ones are asleep.

It's our moment.
Immortalize us.
Cameras are vampires.
You can rewrite history
but you can't touch memory.
Memory has no boundaries.
Truth breaks boundaries.

Five AM.
Same dream.
Lost apartments,
abandoned rooms.
Why didn't I
stay on 4th Street?
Why didn't I
stay?

Another April approaches.
I write a poem each morning.
Won't kill myself
for 30 days
or more.

But a poem is not important.
It's just a goddamned poem.

It doesn't matter if it's a bad poem
because I have a cool leather jacket.
With fringe.

And it doesn't matter if I'm lying
cause I've got shades on.

And it doesn't matter if my imagery
is black & white & grey
cause I've got tattoos.
In color

This is Poetry.
Words don't matter.
I'm a poet.
I don't matter.

I just write.

I write stuff because I've got no stuff,
or I've got too much stuff.
It doesn't fit in my head.
My hard drive is full.

I write stuff because I can't sing
or play the bass guitar.
Where else will I put my stuff
if I don't write it?

I don't write stuff so I won't kill myself.
Suicide isn't that simple.
Writing isn't that helpful.

I've got no balance,
or I'd ride a Harley
down to Daytona.

Instead, I sit
on the back and observe.

I've got no conversation.
Instead, I lean against walls
and observe.

And this is Poetry
And this is not Poetry.

The beautiful poets are everywhere.
The smart ones are asleep.

Where I'm From —East 10th Street Summer

In the summer,
somebody always
sets some speakers
on the windowsill
Sounds of Willie
and Hector
fill the streets

We dance
in the coolness
of fire hydrants
Abuelas rest
their folded arms
on pillows,
keeping one eye
on the pots,
the other on the street,
throw down change
for icies

Tamarindo
Mango
Papaya
Piraguas in large
triangular cone
shaped cups

Louie sells cerveza
on credit
Ephram's got the best
nickel bag
on the block
It's mother's day
and everyone's
got money

and we were happy
There was no word
for homeless
Everyone was home

In 6 floor walk-ups,
toilets in halls,
bathtubs in kitchens,
buildings so old
if you plugged in
an a/c the entire block
went out

Everyone was home

Families escaped the heat,
slept on rooftops,
kids tied to their waists
Marriages began and ended
on front stoops
The West Village
was another country,
a pack of cigarettes
cost two bucks
and all the bodegas
sold loosies

And nobody
was homeless
Wherever we were
we were always home

Everyone was home.

Youngblood Sister
—for Jon

5 flights over 10th Street,
behind window gates
and a police lock,
I lived-
bathtub in the kitchen,
red wood floors, brick walls,
police lock, window gates

I slept
in a loft bed;
above my head
a poem was written
in neat block letters:

Youngblood Sister
you who are older than I
your eyes dark with stories untold
you leap across rooftops fly over fences
your hips move in the night
poems sing in your head
but are your hands quick enough
to stop the knife that will
slash your pretty cheek?
little Youngblood Sister
I want to walk you home
you just run away laughing
quick but not quick enough

I lost the poem
in a fire
and the writer
to a bullet
He held the gun
in the same

shaking hand
that touched me
the night
he named me
his Youngblood Sister.

Here Is What You Don't Know

Before your favorite bar closed
There was a village
Before you cried over Benny's
Burritos or Kim's Video
There was a village

Shoemakers
An egg store
A pork store
Fruit stands
filled with Macintosh
apples and coconuts
There was no kale

There was a village

We played our numbers
on 11th street
Bought umbrella strollers
on Avenue A
When a toddler
tripped on a crack
hands reached out
and caught him
Abuelas babysat,
elbows on pillows
We spent our days
in the park
It was hot inside
Our kids ran laughing
through the sprinklers
We drank beer
through a straw

There was life

before the buildings burned
There was a village

Here is what you don't know

A fire on 10th Street, 4AM
I lived on the fifth floor
Little Bit banged on my door
She was alone with the kids,
hers and Diane's
Sometimes they'd both
go out and leave me the keys
Single mothers did that then

But on the night of the fire
Little Bit was home
The trumpet player in 2C
had nodded out with a cigarette
and died in the blazing heat
He was on methadone, always
triple digits back then
Worse than dope, but legal

Little Bit handed me Santino
We threw blankets over the boys
and raced down the stairs
The banisters were in flames
We ran through the fire, kids
in our arms,
and safely made it to the street
A month later, I threw my furniture
over the connected roof tops
and moved to the 6th floor
right next door

Our disasters were not far
removed from our norms
Buildings burned to the ground

every day
In most cases it was not the fault
of a jazz musician and his cigarette
Every day families disintegrated
Every day tenements made room
for the newcomers who would
arrive a few decades later
Skeletons occupied the streets
where we once lived

We were families
The newer kids, like us,
didn't come here to be artists
Artists were people from Scarsdale
or West 10th Street
We didn't know why we were here
We didn't know why we were anywhere
No philosophy, no flags to wave
We were already artists
But we didn't know that either
No purpose, no reason
Random movements
in the moment

Nobody grew up ice-skating
Nobody took a dance class
Nobody had a bank account
Our money was in our shoe
Same place we always kept it

We made our own language,
dead now to all but a few,
alive in bones arthritic
from too many beatings
or nights out in the cold

Just a few of us left,
speaking in tongues

Here is what you don't know

There was life
before the buildings burned
There was a village.

Walls

Post Woodstock
After the mud and the blood and the beer
And Jimi playing the Star-Spangled Banner
as the son came up and my future husband
in his Motherfucker colors stood with his arm
around his chick coming down from acid
thinking he'd found it, he'd live another day
And the revolution... well, it won't happen fast

It could take five years...

Five years later, and we were just there
Believing in nothing, no reason to be there,
no reason to be, we had nowhere else to go...

Nobody knew where we were;
homeless was a rooftop, not a diagnosis

My friend Belinda got raped three times in one day
She said the last time was the one that really fucked her up–
which meant the first two weren't all that bad,
just what we had come to expect

Before punks and mohawks and crusties
we were just there–
without keys or food stamps
Rape was a part of street life
Prostitution was a four-syllable word

Cut a hole in a red plaid blanket
Call it a winter coat, free stores
and buckskin, not about style,
not about nothing, the NY Dolls
played and it was cool, but
we were just there

Call it what you like
At some point it was over,
the leaders climbed mountains
and threw reels of ticker tape,
and a few of us got to grow up,
rub sun streaks onto broken skin,
and a few of us froze to death,
and a few of us were still just there,
smiling into cameras with broken teeth
and no eyes, feeling like aliens
at weddings and holiday parties

My scars trickle silently along my arms
in random patterns, I remember
every story, but no longer tell

Don't look at me
with your sad eyes

How can I ever explain?

When I lie in bed at night,
listening to rain or traffic noise,
I am struck almost senseless
by the coolness of the sheets,
the safety of my concrete walls.

For Annie

Because you are the last one, the only one to tell it

It no longer matters who cares and maybe nobody reads it anyway,
or maybe it saves a life later on, maybe it's that one kid, just the one kid,
who decides not to believe that short good-looking bearded guy,
and instead of following him, he tells him to fuck off, fuck the fuck off,
but the bottom line is nobody knows, nobody remembers when we
were there, just there, forgetting how to want, moments so powerful
they'd knock a Buddhist out, no need to meditate on impermanence,
we knew there was nothing stronger than the wind at our backs
yet still, a little bit, we believed in better, and less is more, living
in the negative space this country had left us, crossing state lines
with guns and babies, growing old, just a few left, broken bones
never set right, arthritis at 50, nobody's got a full set of teeth and
most of us can't hear right either, on the rare occasions we need
to, but we can read, somebody's kid will read it and show somebody
else's kid, somebody will know, somebody someday will tell all
the charismatic leaders in their leather and jeans to fuck the fuck off.

Final Frontiers

Long ago, on a downtown street
We were small and silly enough to believe
      that it would happen
           Something would happen

Today, we face the final frontier
Lost in the woods   Trees unite against us
Old is an epithet, no longer a state of honor

This is a very small poem, almost as small
        as we were

Tumbling down stairs, jumping from cars
Who would believe us now? Only the ones
      who ran fast, ran by our sides

Standing still, walking backwards
      Turning inward, pushing outward
          Which is better?
              Does anything make sense?

This is a very small poem, as we were
                    once

No mention of prisons, oppression, murder,
        lives that matter, lives unlived

A story told by someone once small and still so silly,
      silly enough to believe
          it would happen,
              to believe in something, anything

Anorexia preferable to the moving hand

There is not enough Botox in the world

                  to make me visible to the naked eye

Not enough drink or drug to crush the lingering
        belief, lying dormant beneath the words
                          behind the sound

Just a taste, small as a mustard seed, as they used to say

Bigger than a fistful, less an idea than an image,
            not yet a memory, no longer a dream

Just a taste, just a smell, of a very small poem.

Waves of New York Poets

Here I am at 7:06 PM standing on line outside the Poetry Project

It's a mild October evening barely crisp enough for a leather jacket
    over a Keith Richards shirt

Doors at 7:30, line stretches around corners, I need a front row seat
    I don't always hear so well these days

We are celebrating Eileen Myles, I remember taking her book home
    from   the Neither/Nor Bookstore on 6th Street, entranced
        by her handsome tomboyish looks
        her white shirt rolled to the elbows,
        her jeans so ripped and faded you could feel the softness

The slight hint of a mullet in a Ramones sort of way, arms crossed
    yet still approachable and on the back cover in that same shirt
        lighting a cigarette,
        Budweiser and pack of Marlboros on the desk,
        brick walls and a typewriter, yes, a typewriter

I don't remember whether I ever paid Rick for the book, probably not

After all, it was 1981 and I never paid for anything and it strikes me
    that few of the chattering girls around me were alive in 1981

I don't remember much about 1981 but I do remember a typewriter
    on a kitchen table and I remember Bimbo Rivas and Pedro Pietri
        shouting poems in the street but maybe I don't remember

Maybe I don't remember if I was really there or thought I must have
    been there because I must have been somewhere, isn't
        everyone? Always?

Here I am at 7:18 PM and the line stretches around two corners
    I'm pretty sure I am where I stand and

       not somebody else I used to know
       as the girls chatter and the boys shuffle their feet

All of the girls are pretty but aren't all young girls pretty?
       Was I? Or was I somebody else even then?

I can't see him but I'm sure Pedro's long coat touched the ground
       when he stooped down to catch that last can of beer
       as it rolled from the brown paper bag

I remember the poet's young sisters laughing as they recalled
       Bimbo's voice so loud in the park he shook the trees

Maybe it was a night I wasn't there..I was somewhere, but I can still
       see the bandshell where the homeless slept, where my daughter
       learned to climb stairs but it's not there anymore and neither
       are Bimbo or Pedro or the poet with the laughing sisters

But somehow, I am, without reason or a hat, I am

And here I am, it's 7:27 PM outside the St. Mark's Church
       In three minutes, doors will open and several hours from now
       the doors will close

I'll leave by myself, remaining who I am, walk down Second Avenue
       across Seventh Street, past the park, and two, no three,
       places I've lived

Past the invisible bandshell, and the silent voices of grown children

Here I am, it is 7:30 PM and the line moves and we start to advance
       just a little bit, just a little bit, we move forward

And Still Just There

And we were there
We were still just there
His name no longer stamped
on crumbling brick walls,
covered now with band
posters, photos of newcomers
in costume, ripped up on
the outside, and we were
there, torn up on the inside,
cool or not, no longer mattered
same loft bed, same police lock,
same tenement steps, we
were just there, invisible even
to one another, rooftops empty,
we watched the parade from
the same stoops, wore the same
tight jeans, slit at the bottom,
the same curly hair that never
hung straight, minimum wage
and welfare checks, six flights
up and no way out, we were just
there and what we didn't know
was that we would never find
a way to live without each other

And we were just there.
To the end. We were there.

Leonard Cohen Inspirations
(Why doesn't the world work for me? – LC, Beautiful Losers)

What kept me here,
tied to the asphalt,
hearts of gravel?

My friends fled to California
or Long Island marriages
College degrees
Teepees
Amsterdam, Africa, Antigua

Where nothing matters but the wind
Everything you need on your back
If you couldn't carry it you didn't need it
Eat whatever's put before you
If there are no forks use a spoon
Or your hands
The food doesn't care
It's as free as dying
Where nothing matters
except for that last breath

But I stayed with you
on Tenth Street
Fire escapes
and police locks
Ford to NY: Drop Dead
We laughed
The lilacs did not grow for us *

Stomped into the floor,
slammed through walls
Yet still the sun rises
and at night
there are stars

In grief, we are empty windows
Crying at noon
on a June downtown day
Walking through parks
Sitting on picnic tables
People passing by,
going to work or lunch
Nobody could see us
I couldn't understand
how the world went on
Planets revolving
Orbiting
Didn't the world know?
Was everybody invisible?
Or was it just us?

I forgot your eyes
I forgot your hands
I forgot the feel
of everything stopping
The universe on pause
You forgot that we have no chance
It can take a lifetime
To find what you cannot have
We are his beautiful losers
Asking Leonard

Why doesn't the world work for us?

*Leonard Cohen, Beautiful Losers

End of the World

End of the world is beginning on Grand
Tall skinny girls, yogurt stand
Pop-up gallery, indie band
End of the world beginning on Grand

It's not the East Village, it's the Lower East Side
It's not the East Village, it's the Lower East Side

Where my father was born, where my grandmother died
She was coming up the steps on East Broadway
Never made it to the top, I pass it every day
My kids can't live where they used to play
The old disappeared and the new have their way

Cause it's the end of the world
Beginning on Grand

My father was born on Avenue C
I always lived east of the DMZ
Copped my bags on the Mighty D
And Avenue B was the place to be
Avenue B was the place to be

And it's the end of the world
Beginning on Grand
Pop-up gallery, Yogurt stand
Five-dollar coffee, indie band
End of the world
Beginning on Grand

Now there's a Holiday Inn on Delancey Street
Used to be a place where the junkies meet
If you didn't come correct you were gonna get beat
Now there's a Holiday Inn on Delancey Street
A Holiday Inn on Delancey Street

It's not the East Village
It's the Lower East Side
Good Friday processions
Chinese French fries
Projects bodegas
Speakers on the sills
Kids in wheelchairs
Fire drills

And the End of the world
It's beginning on Grand
Five-dollar coffee yoghurt stands
Tall skinny girls, indie bands
End of the world beginning on Grand.

Jeanette Powers

Water Is a Woman

water is a woman see how she fits
into whatever vessel you devise for her
watch her overflow
watch her evaporate away
you must vacuum seal her
to keep her tight in your jar

watch her grow green and brown
with primordial life, with algae
watch the amoeba bloom of her surface
soon she becomes murky with life
she cannot help but bear fruit
concocting children is her day job
and everything needs her

water is a woman look how she persists
corrosive and tenacious above everything
her carving the Ozark caves deep
across the southwest plateau
her body is a canyon of flood and rush
she pours herself downstream
relentless as hunger
graceful as mercy
she doesn't take the high road
she takes the path of least resistance

watch her stay low
and curving always with the hips of the land
the cliffs open to her as she angles her way home
always home to the great source
the shared genesis of life
ocean and current and womb

a woman is an ocean look how vast
she persists against the rat tooth of shore

in small swells and carousing squall
thrusting a legion of hurricanes
she cannot be moved, really
by any whim but her own

water is a woman in blue and clear
neither a dark cloud or a silver lining
but something yearning to fall
each drop of her rain
each catapulting globe is a perfect
reflection of the entire world

Newton's Second Law

I used to do a lot of things without you
like dancing in the living room
and making three-course meals
with just one plate, one candle,
one Moon.

I'd watch the clouds hide
and think of you being hidden too
sometimes it was as though
a single day took a lifetime
but then suddenly months and years
were gone before a single dish was done
and it felt like all the songs were over
like all the music was gone
and I held absolutely still
no pressure, no motion, no me.

Because without you is a hollow
is an aperture with no end
waiting for you
I am less than a wisp
I am currentless
I can't even be detected
because without you
there is only absence.

Hearts Break All the Time

I remember the gnarled hands
of my grandfather
working the rotary dial
of the old goldenrod yellow
Ma Bell telephone
calling the hospital
where my grandmother lay
waiting to have her chest cracked
for a double bypass
heartbreak was not new to her

I hung my fingertips
on the tall bureau with the phone
and the lazy susan with her fake pearls
watching him talk and listening
I love you, Helen
I'd never heard him say that before
tears fell down through the stubble of his cheeks
they were the bluest eyes I've ever seen
his hand always trembled for a cigarette
and it did then too
they are decades gone now
just like land lines and my youth

the doctor is earnest
reading my genome results
tells me I can't absorb folic acid
or Vitamin D, my liver is weak
and that no matter how healthy I am
a heart attack is sure

I've already had several
I assure her with a smile

she doesn't laugh
but I'm hoping I'm just like my grandmother.

Reflections in the Windows of Your First Car

With my first driver's license
and the 5-speed shifter
of a gold 1984 Plymouth Turismo
gripped in my hands
I drove out of the suburbs
and into the big city
knowing nowhere to go.

Grinding gears through Raytown
passing the long sewer of Brush Creek
I found myself in Midtown Kansas City
took a left on 39th Street from Main
and flashing lights pulled me
into the bank parking lot
immediately.

I didn't know what to do
when justice is demanded
I popped out of the car
and just began to beg
it's my first day driving
my mom will kill me
I promise it won't happen again.

Then I catch a glimpse of myself
in the reflection of the window
and see my face covered
in armadillo stamps
from goofing around
with Sam after school,
who we, of course, all called Scooby.

My heart falls out, because I think
no one looking so foolish
will ever get out of anything

could never be taken seriously
and I surrender myself to my fate
look the officer straight in the eye
and just say, I'm sorry.

He pats me on the shoulder
and laughs, be more careful next time
and drives away, I watched that man
choose mercy over justice
two decades later, I still think of him
and the power of an honest apology
every nowhere I go.

Brother D

The first time he held a gun he was eleven.
He was the man of the house now.
It would be decades before
he learned what it meant to be a man,
he tells me in the observation car
watching the barren trees flashing
he's on his way home.

It's eleven years sober in Erie
where he wears a blue coat
and calls on schools
taking guns out of children's hands
and being the father he never had.

He says, there was no one to look after me
of course I fell apart.

Of course, of course.

delta heart equals zero

The arch of your sneer is
remarkable
it turns me into
a world-class circus performer
I contort, I please
I trapeze, I elephant
I balance on the ball
with my red nose
and you laugh

no you don't laugh.

You are an all-star pitcher
and I can't home run
the brutal speed
of your silent
treatment
I just hold up
this mirror
and we are both broken

you know we are both broken.

I fell from the trapeze
I broke my leg sliding into home
I need what I can't ask for
but I can't find a way there

can you?

All I have to give is
no change of heart
I am an immovable object
you'll be sick of me first
so snag a tooth on my lip

break my arm in half
I'll grow all new body parts
you spit in my face
I drink your water

never leaving is my only gift.

Runaway with the Circus
—for Michael Morales

We drank wine from the bottle
in front of the bookstore
while he guessed the name
of my dead father
from the way
my eyelids twitched
while he said the alphabet.

I sang him row row row your boat
backwards while we stumbled
up 39th Street to his apartment
and climbed the ivy trellis
onto the back porch
because both of us
enjoy
doing things wrong.

He ran away to the circus
when he was 17 years old
and never went home again
dream a but is life.

I took off my shirt
and without hesitation
laid down on his bed
of nails
he hollered *noooooo!*
but something inside of me
knew exactly how to do it
without ever being told.

Once you decide to commit
do it with your whole being
don't hesitate or take a small bite

move softly and breathe calmly
stream the down gently
distribute your weight evenly
and then
enjoy
the thousand points
they feel like kisses
merrily merrily merrily.

Snippets of Poems that Didn't Make It into Poems

Are you nervous to see me?
Not as nervous as I am that I might
never see you again.

I can't tell you how to wake up like this
with jingle bells in my asshole
and twerking with the birds.

The intensity of indifference.

We can always see our breath in the air here
in Toledo to stay warm we must
stand in front of the bathroom space heater
stay snuggled in bed or drive
gasoline is cheaper than electricity here
I say why do we call it gas when it's a liquid
you say lotta things don't make sense.

He held a gun for the first time at eleven years old.

(actually that one might make it)

Queers in myths, Becky in a hat.

Alarmingly catholic.

Can I heal your face?

Poems to needle Mimi, they are not about knitting.

Why don't I have a spare tire?

She said *You are my oldest friend*
but I don't know how to be one
I said *People have been beating*

on us our whole lives.

Sasquatch vs. Chupacabra.

A dog that taught me loyalty
and kept me playing
a dog I got for my inner child
who protected me so many years
and we ran creeks in floods
chased armadillos out from rotting logs
and were never alone together.

Sometimes you just need an extra hour of sleep
with your head resting gently on a chest
warm, heartbeat slow, steady, going nowhere.

Wish we were all tourists
just here to see the sights.

I never met a free cow once
only jailed cows.

The grief of an uninspired kiss.

No condolences, only fishing tips.

How We Move on
     —for Jeremiah Walton

Baby Bear is a dirty kid who uses my backyard firepit
to burn his journals in a Ceremony of Passage

We haven't invented new mythologies for centuries
and they become my first Vestal Virgin, a living altar

to the Nows of Travel and Homecoming and How
To Let Things Go That Once Were a Story Made of Iron

How do we change the way we worship and murder
Who can let me arise from the Mist without chains

His pages float, charring up into the wind and are caught
on thermals, a memory glows then turns to ash

I watch from the Kitchen Window, still covered in ice
along the edges, I grow colder with distance

There's an empty leash on the porch tied to a hand-woven rope
that used to keep my dog from running off with the neighbors

I try not to think of my inner child dying with that dog
I invent that his death doesn't kill my longing to play and be loyal

Baby Bear adds another book to the fire, it falls open
and the edges of the paper burn to the center

We are both shivering.

Some Quick of Hope

the river is sweet tea and way high
and although it's one hundred and five
the humidity makes it feel like hell blew through
and found it couldn't take the heat

but the water is cold from last night's hard rain
and the only way to survive getting in
is to do it all at once, surrender with breath held
and this is how we dive in and come up again

the river is for letting go the sweat of the cage
is the place for inventing what comes next
and here is where we come together to decide
how and what we name the unknown future

why the cost of starting over is so steep
and who the ghosts keep haunting day in and out
while the current keeps each of every us
newly touched and baptized clean

there's no two ways around this river
only one way down and no way out
before we cross her with pennied eyes
to some sort of wet heaven we haven't yet dreamt

95 is Still an A
—for Kyle J. Osborne

None of us have bowling shoes
which turns out not to matter
since Wednesday nights are league nights
at Thunder Alley in Owensville, Missouri
which makes us just an audience tonight.

Eight lanes and eight teams
carhartts, plaid flannels, ball caps with fishhooks
and one t-shirt that says normal people scare me
I immediately call dibs on him
he's the youngest bowler and his swing
is like a pendulum keeping time for giants.

Many beer bellies on floating feet
doing a ballroom dance for strikes
none of them can catch a spare to save their life
but Cassie brings more pitchers of Bud Light
and takes the pinches on the butt with a laugh
she doesn't blush because she's the only one
making any money tonight.

Wings are fifty cents, and plenty hot
they serve non-alcoholic Busch Light
and the claw machine is still a rip off
Brad behind the bar is a clutz
who spills the tip jar into the trash can
and we're laughing at him
behind our hands
and the pins on the lanes
are hit dead on and crashing
and it sounds good to everyone's ears.

Finally, Kyle begs a lane off the owner
since one team finished their game early

his form is perfect, with that one long leg
going out like a ballet dancer behind him
though his face is sour and apologetic
as he rolls the last gutter ball
but reminds us: 95 is still an A.

Never Turn Down a Glass of Sweet Tea
—for Jason Baldinger

not everyone can weigh the difference
between cheesecake with strawberry or chocolate
in a single heartbeat and just go with one
or the other

very few people will just walk into nowhere
and not really care whether or not they get where
they are going because part of them already believes
they are exactly where they should be

many people lost their fathers to embarrassing deaths
and go on to live and tell the tale over cheap beers
in backwater pool halls where the bartender
wears a face of knowing loss

only you shared a glass of sweet tea with me
fried okra and calamity pressing at future windows
where we promised that if only we could figure it all out
we'd share that with each other, too

Old Dogs

We meet at a kitchen table
and sit at opposite ends
it is not your table, or mine
there is a rotting lemon
dessicated ginger root

all things grow old.

This table doesn't get much use
outside of our meeting here
you cook up stories of Toledo
your grandfathers and death
I tell you about dandelions
and how I think of you
as the one we saw
popping from under the snow
the day we walked
to the cemetery.

Which is not our graveyard, either
but a borrowed valentine
with an old dog chasing a squirrel
he'll never catch again
since his knees gave out
and we both know something
about how the body
can't anymore.

We go out to eat yesterday
and today and don't talk about
tomorrow, ever
your right hand palsies still
both of mine are growing surely
into the shape of my grandmothers'
in our eyes are tombstones

but we are holding hands.

Sister, Sing Me
—for Jessica Ayala

Sister, sing me the mountain song
of your ancestors
who know how the tear falls
from the stone and why the ocean
heals our troubled hearts
who take the arrows from the quiver
and transform them into lilies
and the arrowhead of family.
The song is behind your ears
which carry light air of the Andes
deep sediment of kingfisher and toucan
your eyes speak the chiming breath
of a kiss on the forehead
your ancestors trust you with the secret
names of planets pulling you into the future
they know your strength when you do not.
You are sent to a foreign hemisphere
with your braids pleated panther sleek
with drumbeat rising in your tongue
and a language beyond the cliff and delta
yours is a song of salt and net and trill
you heave under the weight of life
until you sweat under the medicine feather
the peak of the summit is your gift to give.

Cycles of Grief Go on and on

In no good world is it right
for a mother to leave behind
two young boys when she dies
or for the family to fight
over her crumbs, her car
the paint by number of a white horse
the hand-painted sculpture
of a monkey, hanging
from a real rope
the raining oil lamp
with the naked woman inside
there's no justice
in fighting over her wedding ring
while those two boys
sit in pews praying
for their mom.

There is no kindness in giving
your queer granddaughter
a bible for graduation
after fifteen years of her
hiding behind the pulpit
knowing she can't be baptized
into the faith of her family
and cutting off her college fund
when she's caught red-handed
with a woman at the movie theater
then sending her out into the world
without a safety net
unable to pray without
remembering being cast away.

For the abandoned
it feels like everyone
is beating on them for their whole lives

and they are the only ones paying the price
it seems like everyone
is just getting away with so much cruelty
dressed up as the Christian thing to do
and we, abandoned through grief,
loss, through being different
find our own solace
and too often in razor blades,
another dozen bottles
always bashing our heads
in prayer against a wall.

Are we raising a generation
of hungry ghosts, sleeping
with clenched fists, ready to punch back
at first waking, unable to be given
an apology they can hear
every reason just an excuse
always believing everyone
is going to be right at our throats
the second we show our self
our rage an impacted tooth
our memory a suppurating ulcer
the only cheek turned, always our own?

After Bouguereau's *The Bathers*

Don't forget how to listen
or if you have
drop everything and run
to a sandbar in a river
you'll prolly have to swim

take off your shoes before you leave
take off your clothes before you get there

it will be chill and brisk
there will be fish who nibble
the round peach fuzz of your bare thighs
and toes and elsewhere, too
let them

be quiet
remember you know where you are
this is it
remember you know how to breathe

yes, fresh, yes
your body grows heavy
you stop holding yourself up so much
you put your mind in its own pocket

you are hear
you are here

lay on the sand and spread your legs
show the sun your whole body
there is no shame

the heron flies over you
the warbler continues her lunch
deep sip fresh water across the way

and a salamander rests near your foot

you are part of this
your body will always remember
but you will always have to remind your mind

> *happiness is light as a feather*
> *but none can bear it*
> *calamity is heavy as the earth*
> *yet none can avoid it*

there will be another storm
but right now
you stand naked
before everything there is
and all is right with the world.

(italicized lines from the Inner Chapters of the Tao)

BORSENIK

Dianne Borsenik is active in the northern Ohio poetry scene and regional reading circuit; she recently featured in "We're No Angels" (Speak of the Devil, Lorain, Ohio) and "2 Chefs & a Beat: Poetic Justice Edition" (Porco Lounge and Tiki Room, Cleveland, Ohio). Her work has appeared in numerous journals and anthologies, including *Chiron Review, Main Street Rag, Resurrection River Poems* (Wick Poetry Center, 2019) and *A Rustling and Waking Within* (Ohio Poetry Association, 2017); recent books include *Raga for What Comes Next* (Stubborn Mule Press, 2019), and *Age of Aquarius* (Crisis Chronicles Press, 2017). Actor Jonathan Frid used three of her poems in his live show *Genesis of Evil*, and Lit Youngstown printed her poem "Disco" on their tee shirts, which makes her feel like a rock star. Borsenik is editor/publisher at NightBallet Press, and lives in Elyria, Ohio. Find her on Facebook and at www.dianneborsenik.com.

Acknowledgments:

Grateful acknowledgment is given to the following publications in which these poems first appeared.

Guttural Magazine — Wearing Mail
Oct Tongue 2 (Crisis Chronicles Press, 2017) — Aurora Borealis
The Ramingo's Porch — Spring Fever

Author's note:

Anomalies in the Garden and Psalmodies in Vitro contain separate, nested poems within them. The titles of the hidden poems are Heart Sounds and Eden Star.

Author's Statement:

A number of these poems hold hands with sex, drugs, and rock & roll in an unabashed nod to the author's hippie heart.

COOK

Juliet Cook's poetry has appeared in a small multitude of magazines. She is the author of numerous poetry chapbooks, recently including *From One Ruined Human to Another* (Cringe-Worthy Poets Collective, 2018), *DARK PURPLE INTERSECTIONS (inside my Black Doll Head Irises)* (Blood Pudding Press for Dusie Kollektiv 9, 2019), and *Another Set of Ripped-Out Bloody Pigtails* (The Poet's Haven, 2019). She also another chapbook forthcoming, *the rabbits with red eyes* (forthcoming from ethel).

Cook's first full-length individual poetry book, *Horrific Confection* was published by BlazeVOX. Her more recent full-length poetry book, *A Red Witch, Every Which Way*, was a collaboration with j/j hastain published by Hysterical Books in 2016. Her most recent full-length individual poetry book, *Malformed Confetti* was published by Crisis Chronicles Press in 2018.

Cook also sometimes creates abstract painting collage art hybrid creatures.

Find out more at julietcook.weebly.com

Acknowledgements:

Many of these poems (sometimes in slightly different variations) have previously appeared in various literary magazines (some of which are now defunct) and/or other sources, as noted below. Thank you kindly to all of the editors involved in these projects.

"Batter Up" appeared in *Queen of Cups*

"Doll Blood Splattering" appeared in *The Rising Phoenix Review*

"Unfriend Everyone" appeared in *Red Fez*

"What Good Does the Truth Do?" appeared in *The Chaotic Review*

"I Need To Bow My Head and Say Your Prayers Even If I Don't Believe in You" appeared in *Full of Crow*

"My tendency to feel as if expressing myself is wrong" appeared in *Rag Queen Periodical*

"Not a Member of Your Snake Handling Church Organ" appeared in *Octopus Review*

"Flying Snake" appeared in *Masque & Spectacle*

"Dark Light" appeared in *Black Poppy Review*

"When I was a little girl, I threw a rock at a crab and accidentally killed it" appeared in *Really System*

"Bloodlines" appeared in *Arsenic Lobster* - and also appeared within Cook's chapbook *From One Ruined Human to Another* (Cringe-Worthy Poet's Collective, 2018)

"Out of Control" appeared in *White Stag Publishing*

"Dropping Point" appeared in *Moon Cycle*

"Root Rot" appeared in *Riot Felice* - and also appeared within Cook's chapbook *From One Ruined Human to Another* (Cringe-Worthy Poet's Collective, 2018)

"You pull your latest force field out and shoot another load" appeared in *Thank You for Swallowing*

"Ripped Out Red" appeared in *Menacing Hedge*

"Inside an Old Basement" appeared in *Picaroon Poetry*

PERL

Puma Perl is a widely published poet and writer, as well as a performer and producer. She is the author of two chapbooks, *Ruby True* and *Belinda and Her Friends*, and two full-length poetry collections, *knuckle tattoos*, and *Retrograde*, (great weather for MEDIA.) A fifth, *Birthdays Before and After* (Beyond Baroque) is due for release in 2019. She is the creator, curator, and producer of Puma Perl's Pandemonium, which launched at the Bowery Electric in 2012 and brings spoken word together with rock and roll. As Puma Perl and Friends, she performs regularly with a group of excellent musicians. She's received two honorable mentions and one first place award from the New York Press Association in recognition of her journalism and was the recipient of the 2016 Acker Award in the category of writing; she lives and works on the Lower East.

A comprehensive list of video links and updates on events can be found on her blog: pumaperl.blogspot.com

Acknowledgments:

WHERE I'M FROM - EAST 10TH STREET SUMMER | *knuckle tattoos*, Erbacce Press

YOUNGBLOOD SISTER | 2010, Erbacce Press, UK

POWERS

Jeanette Powers is a writer-artist, working-class anarchist and listener of rivers and bats. They mess around, mostly, and have a hard time doing anything that doesn't bring joy. Powers is a founding editor of Stubborn Mule Press and an organizer for FountainVerse: KC Small Press Poetry Fest. They are also an art barista for Fictional Cafe and the singular subversive voice of Spartan Press' developmental editing. JP and JR make most of their decisions tits deep in the Gasconade River. What else? Their gender identity is currently *holy person* and their dog died this year which still hurts brutally. This book is for *Ollymas*. @dada_ahha and jeanettepowers.com

Acknowledgments:

Water Is a Woman | *Winedrunk Sidewalk*

Newton's Second Law | "After the Flood" from Stubborn Mule Press

Reflections ..., Cycles of Grief ... | *As It Ought to Be*

Brother D, Snippets..., Old Dogs | *Former People*

Some Quick of Hope | *The Wild Word*

Never Turn Down a Glass of Sweet Tea | *Rye Whiskey Review*

www.ingramcontent.com/pod-product-compliance
Lightning Source LLC
Chambersburg PA
CBHW020123130526
44591CB00032B/491